This Book Belongs To:

The back of each coloring page is a dark rectangle to prevent colors from bleeding through. This would be a great space for vision boarding. Just clip out and tape or paste images that represent your vision of your future.

I really hope this coloring book provides you with the motivation and stress relief that we can all use right now.

If you enjoy it, please return to Amazon and leave a review. Thanks so much and Happy Coloring!

Copyright ©2020 by Journals by Melody Wynn.
All Rights Reserved.

You Deserve

A Raise!

I Never Fail!

I Learn & I Grow

Your Strength Is Greater Than Your Struggle!

Choose

Happiness

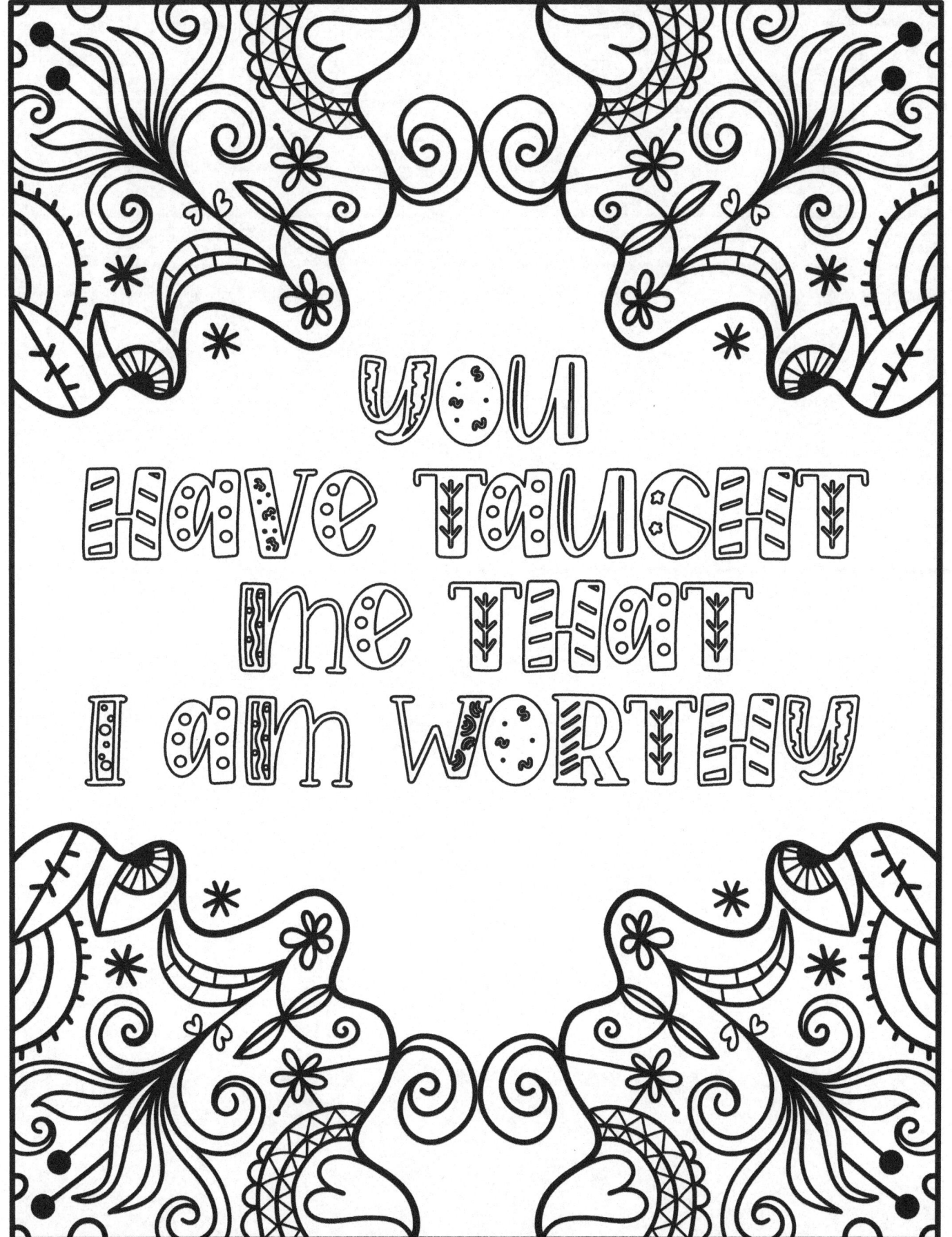

You Help Me To Be Open

To New Ideas

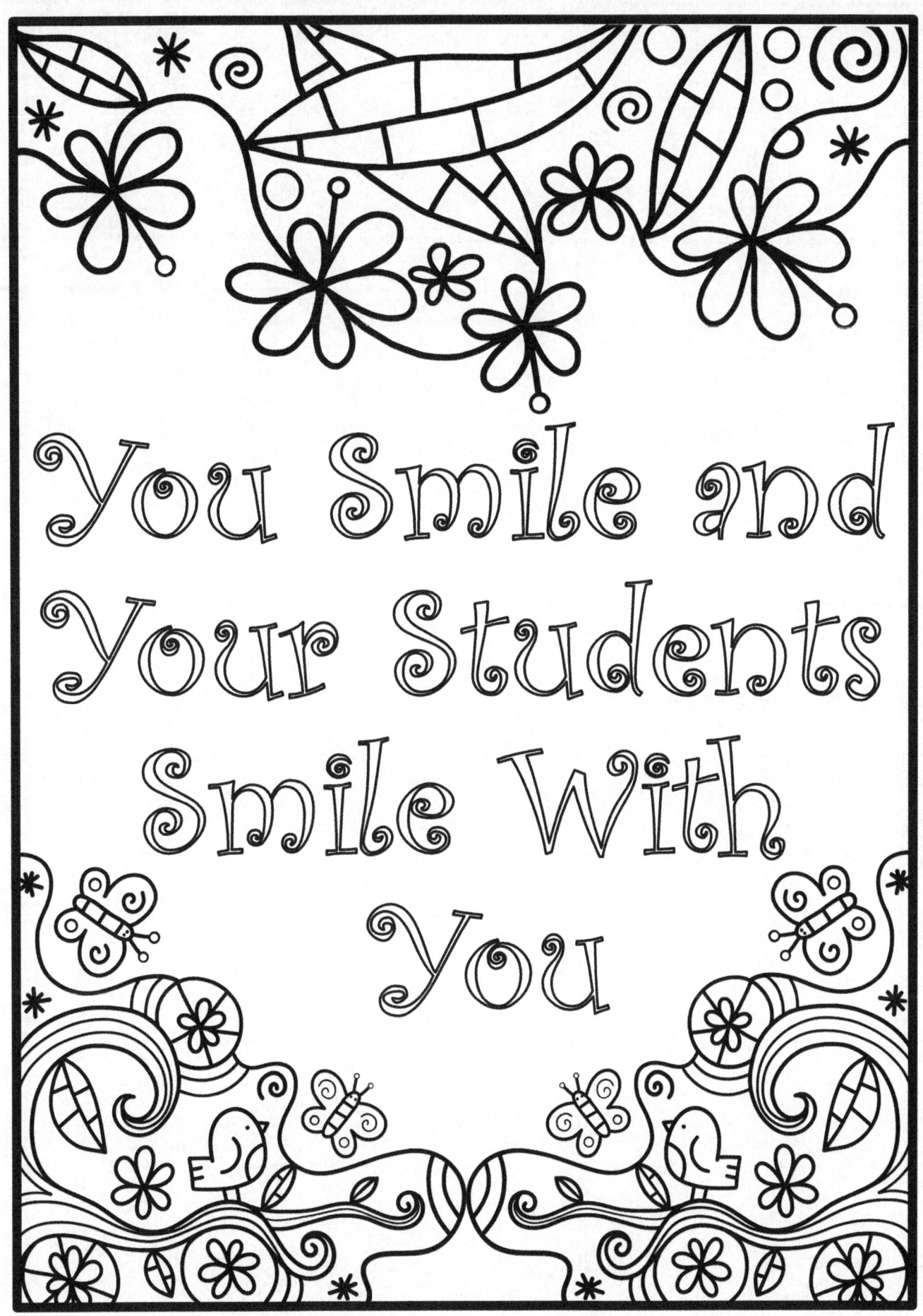

Teaching Is Hard Because It Matters

To Teach Is To Love

Strive For Progress Not Perfection

Made in the USA
Las Vegas, NV
06 June 2022